May your life

Extraordinary Detour

A storm raged the day my husband died and went to heaven the first time.

Sometimes, scary detours can be extraordinary miracles in disguise.

By

God bless you,

Penelope Silvers

Penelope

Patrice Schmitt, Editor

PenelopeSilvers.com

ExtraOrdinaryDetour.com

Twitter @Philosbooks

www.PenelopeSilvers.com

Published by: BookBaby
7905 North Route 130, Pennsauken, NJ 08110
www.bookbaby.com * 877-961-6878

ISBN 978-1-66782-868-8

~~~~~

God's ways are not our ways.
The best laid plans go astray.
God's ways are higher than our ways.
God wants what we can't see today.

~~~~~~~

CONTENTS

This book is dedicated to our Heavenly Father
without whom there would be NO extraordinary detours.

Next, a big thank you goes out to all my early supporters
during the Publishizer campaign.

They are truly angels!

Angela
Judy & Ed
Jenny
Liz
Micki
Nicki
Peter
Sharon
Shawn
Delores
My dad (now in heaven)

PART I

Introduction

Extraordinary moments happen to us all—detours that send us off in crazy and unexpected directions. Traveling along life's road, we're thrown off course with no warning and nowhere to turn. We're shocked and frightened, but have no choice but buckle up for the ride of our lives. The story you're about to read is true, although some of the names have been changed.

There's no question these events threatened to drown us as we cried out to God day and night with desperate, anguished prayers. But how can we know the ways of God? His ways are mysterious and deeper than any ocean; we could never plumb the depths. If we knew everything God was doing behind the scenes (if all was revealed to us), we'd never be scared or even have an anxious thought again. Even if the curtain was pulled aside for a tiny peek.

With this in mind, ponder your own life. Are you a spiritual seeker or believer who's lost hope God is faithful and truly cares for you? Think about how you'd react if your worst fears actually came true. How will you press on and keep going?

Moreover, as you read this book, I pray you'll sense the wonder and assurance of heaven. Next, that you'll fully grasp God is on your side and can be trusted amidst your darkness and pain. And finally, you may reflect on your *own* ExtraOrdinary Detour where you sensed God's leading. A new journey—where God was right beside you in the deepest, darkest valleys.

"Once we truly see God at work, we will never be concerned again about the things that happen, because we are actually trusting in our Father in heaven, whom the world cannot see."

~Oswald Chambers, *My Utmost for His Highest*

Beginning

Did you ever have something so amazing—so extraordinary—happen to you that you could not speak of it? Perhaps for fear no one would believe you? Or, perhaps because the event was so special and touched you so deeply you could not even describe it?

Well, my husband did have such an extraordinary event. And he could not speak of it, or perhaps he did not want to—because it was so special he wanted to hold it close—even from me.

He finally shared his experience with me, so I can share it with you.

Helicopter to Heaven

November 13, 2013, started out an ordinary day. But by noon, Ron was aboard an ambulance with sirens blaring.

The local hospital didn't have facilities to handle his massive stroke, so five hours later he was airlifted to Shands Hospital in Gainesville, Florida. Six people shifted him from bed to gurney into an idling ambulance, where he was hustled down the street to a helicopter pad by Cooter Pond. A pilot and nurse awaited his arrival.

Meanwhile, a violent storm raged with gusting winds and slanting rain. The storm rocked the tiny aircraft, and the nurse fretted whether they'd be able to take flight. She had a right to be concerned. Ron, however, was not; for beside him, stood a friend. Soothingly, this friend assured the nurse everything would be alright, and instructed her to get Ron to the hospital.

This friend remained by Ron's side as the helicopter lifted. Ron arose from bed, and his friend ushered him to the window. "Look outside," he said. Ron peered into total blackness. Suddenly, vile and foul words spewed from voices and faces he couldn't see. They ranted on about hating God. Repulsed, a foul, smoky smell assaulted his nostrils. He was amazed by the sights and sounds.

His friend still remained by his side, and Ron returned to the bed.

Quickly, the air trip was over. Through whipping winds, the helicopter arrived safely and landed on Shands' rooftop. Without delay, several waiting hands grabbed the gurney and hurried him downstairs to the emergency room. They knew there was little time to spare—after all, he was dying.

Upon arrival in the ER, with his friend still beside him, Ron's eyes opened to the most breathtaking place he'd ever seen. Nothing like the horrible scene he'd witnessed previously from the helicopter window—the one that assaulted all his senses.

No, this new place definitely eclipsed all seven wonders of the world. People were younger. The music out of this world. Ron grew up loving gospel music, singing, and directing choirs, but nothing compared to this. He was awestruck in wonder at sights he could not describe. Completely happy and totally at peace, he was now in heaven.

Before he could take it all in, God spoke and said, "Ron, you can't stay here. You have to go home."

Ron argued, "But God, this is the most blessed place I've ever seen. It's fantastic! Why can't I stay? I don't want to leave."

God said, "You must go back now."

Confused, Ron could not understand why God would send him back to earth. In a flash, he was back in his body. His friend had disappeared.

Carnival Atmosphere

In the weeks prior, life was a struggle. Despite this, we did what it took to survive, pay bills and put food on the table. We couldn't find paid work despite sending resume after resume, only being called for a trickle of interviews. Making a living in our small town was becoming increasingly difficult. The economy had tanked and Ron had been laid off since 2011. I hadn't worked outside the home in years.

The month of May signaled the beginning of our yard sales. Unemployment compensation dried up, temperatures inched up from mid 80's into 90's, and humidity rolled in like a heavy wet blanket. Depending on how generous people were with their spending, some weeks we'd sell all week, then need to extend sales into the weekend.

Every day was the same. We pulled blue tarps from tables so merchandise was visible, Ron tossed signs into the back of our Blue Pacifica, then drove off to post on several street corners. Processions arrived in the form of trucks, mini vans, economy cars and SUV's, one after another, lining the streets and side of our yard, with people of all shapes, sizes and colors emerging to pick over stuff on display. This relentless stream of bargain-hunting strangers walked up our driveway, trampled our lawn, and picked over small items, haggling over a few pennies or dollars. Many were lonely and stopped by just to shoot the breeze, grateful for a listening ear. Many times I practically gave things away so we had enough for milk, bread, eggs, or gas.

This scene stretched on through the relentless Florida summer into June, July, and August. Sales dried up into September and October, when children returned to school, and parents now put their money towards sports equipment, books, and music lessons. Truthfully, we were partly relieved.

A Stinking Mess

Cooler winter weather arrived in November. Ron still posted pink and neon green signs, and processions of cars and people still appeared. Our yard and driveway were still dotted with tents and tables.

The prior weekend had been sultry—perfect conditions for the emergence of Lovebugs. What a lovely name! However, try to imagine a swarm of any kind of bug. They emerged overnight and multiplied like a plague, sticking to a car's body, front grill, and windshield and if not cleaned immediately, bodily fluids eat off paint. A member of the family of march flies, they are also known as the honeymoon fly, kissing bug, or double-headed bug. We just call them extreme pests. The adult is a small, flying insect common to parts of Central America and the southeastern United States, especially along the Gulf Coast. During and after mating, adult pairs remain coupled, even in flight, for up to several days.

Florida heat we could deal with, but add in swarms of bugs, and the conditions for outdoor selling become miserable. Irritated customers swatted aside bugs while shopping. Already wet and dripping from humidity, their thick swarms flew into our faces, sticking in our hair and clothes. Then, finally breathing their last, they died inside mugs and on merchandise. Once the swarm dwindled, it looked like a massacre, with a sea of dead, reeking black bugs everywhere. A disgusting mess.

After any storm, it's clean up time, so we shut down our store for bug patrol. Armed with a vacuum, we worked several hours, delicately sucking up soft bug bodies so as not to squish them. We blew off sale items, and swept the driveway and sidewalk. Just when we thought the work was finished, a bug would appear inside a DVD or up a shirt sleeve.

Our plans were one final blow-out sale, then close up shop for the winter. Heat, humidity, bugs, bending, stretching, lifting and chatting up people for dollars had taken its toll on our aching bodies. Physically and mentally exhausted, we needed a break. The final sale would happen the weekend of November 16, and after that time, unsold items would be brought back in the house or garage, donated or tossed. Merchandise was ready for the weekend, completely covered underneath a large blue tarp in the center of our yard, a small tent in the driveway, and several tables.

The past few months had been very difficult, and we were trying to make sense of it all. In the evening we'd sit together and discuss what we'd been hearing from God separately during our prayer times. We both strongly felt God tugging at our hearts and leading us in another direction. When Ron was younger, he'd had the opportunity to go on a mission trip to Venezuela, but wasn't able to raise enough money. Recently, we'd attended a mission conference at a local church, and brought home brochures on Ecuador. Reading about the Ecuadorians of South America seemed to fan a little flame inside the both of us.

Excited, we began forging new plans. We started researching cheaper places to live from money raised from our sales, and decided we were no longer survival selling. We'd sell everything we owned to make a significant change, and decided to move to South America for a fresh start—and lower cost of living.

The rest of our week was free to do with as we pleased, with no hint of storm clouds brewing on the horizon.

An Ordinary Day

Wednesday, November 13, 2013, dawned like any other day. Sleeping in, we awoke to bright sunlight flickering through bedroom sheers. Breakfast was the usual oatmeal, craisins, apples, and walnuts. A light breeze blew, with the temperature a mild 60 degrees. Sun masked gray clouds forming on the horizon, threatening to roll in later that afternoon. A perfect, Florida winter day.

I made plans for the day. First, was writing, and then we'd drive out to visit a vacant piece of land we were selling. I attempted to work but Ron was pressing my buttons, and I became irritable. Around 11:30 a.m., we sat side by side on the floral couch in my office as I attempted to complete a romance novel in time for Christmas.

He sensed my frustration and attempted to leave, but his path was blocked by a large purple exercise ball. Instead of going around, he fell forward onto the ball—the same one I'd kicked out of the way all week. Strange, since I'm an "everything in its place" kinda gal. He pushed himself up from the ball and left the room.

Puzzled, I followed as he stumbled into his office, knocking over pictures and books. My breath caught in my throat. Sliding my arm through his, I guided him to a blue recliner where he plopped like a rag doll. I tried keeping him engaged asking, "Are you alright?"

His head jerked back and forth, eyes darting left then right. He couldn't focus, but suddenly his head and eyes stopped moving and he caught sight of me. "Oh, there you are!" he said. At this point, his face paled as glassy eyes stared off in the distance—the Ron I knew was gone. Scared, I struggled to breathe and remain calm.

"Something fell," he said with a blank stare. He rose again, weaved through our living room, slammed into bar stools and sent a telescope flying. He made it out the front door and splayed out in a chair—still with that same vacant look.

Shakily, I fired off questions. "How many fingers do I have up? What's your name? What day is this? What year?" His responses were incoherent babbling. I'd read up on this not long before today. Dashing inside, I googled stroke symptoms. Trouble walking. Check. Incoherent speech. Check. Blurred vision or difficulty focusing. Check and check. He could still move his body at that point, so that was crossed off the list. All symptoms were present except for one: numbness on one side of the body.

Rattled, I dialed 911, not thinking clearly when I handed Ron the phone. Of course, he couldn't answer any of the dispatcher's questions. I snatched the phone back and she said, "No, I want YOU to ask him the questions."

We repeated the same list of questions I'd already asked. The only missing test was for him raise his arms. "Honey, raise your arms, please." He could not. Finally, I breathed a sigh of relief when she said the ambulance was on the way. Now that help was coming, he went inside and lay down to sleep.

Lord, help us, please. I followed closely behind.

Battle to Go

Sirens screamed through our neighborhood, abruptly ended at our driveway, and paramedics popped up on our doorstep as if by magic. I was relieved, but one look told me this male and female duo wouldn't be able to handle Ron. He's six foot, seven inches, and these two were each a foot or two shorter.

I ushered them into the bedroom and we gathered around the bed. Wringing my hands, I said, "He won't get up. I'm trying to keep him from falling asleep, but he won't listen." Tears filled my eyes.

"That's normal," he said. "Reasoning with a stroke victim is next to impossible. They're not in their right mind and don't have the ability to understand you."

Despite that, I still continued to try. "Honey, please listen to me. You're having a stroke and need to go to the hospital. These people are here to help, but you must get up and get on the stretcher. If you don't, you could die. Please!"

Ron hugged his pillow tightly, curled into a defiant ball and shouted, "I'm not going anywhere. I'm going to sleep. Leave me alone!" Those words were plain as day despite the other gibberish. The paramedics also tried, but made it clear they weren't going to force him onto the stretcher. My assumption about them was correct.

I tried a different way, appealing to his love for me. Still no response. Time was running out. *Why, oh why, did he have to put on those flimsy gray shorts with the hole right in the crotch?* The paramedics had probably seen it all.

Short man said, "This isn't working, and we're not going to force him. Do you want us to call the Sheriff's office and send for deputies? Sometimes, stroke patients can become violent and they can restrain him."

I didn't want anyone to get hurt. I just wanted my husband to live. "Go ahead and call them," I choked out.

In short order, sheriff's vehicles joined the ambulance. Now, our bedroom overflowed with three uniformed officers, two paramedics—and me—all staring down at Ron. The 10 x 10 room seemed to shrink.

As if nothing had gone on before, Ron suddenly sat up, paused on the edge of the bed and said, "I'm ready to go."

A flurry of activity ensured, as everyone scrambled to attention before he changed his mind. He stood up, and as the paramedics helped him to the edge of the stretcher, his unmentionables showed up right through that hole. *If he knew, he'd be so embarrassed.*

Strapped in, they wheeled him out the front door and into the waiting ambulance. I was to follow. No violence occurred that day, and no guns were drawn. By noon, sirens again blared out of our neighborhood and through town to Citrus Memorial Hospital.

Urgent Prayers

The house was quiet now with Ron aboard the ambulance, and I had a moment to think. My only thought was, *Who can I call to pray with me?* I racked my brain. In between churches, we didn't have any close friends to call.

Then, God gave me a name. Our son's youth pastor from our previous church had been instrumental in teaching our son and taking him on some mission trips. He and his wife were missionaries to Brazil before they accepted the position of youth leaders of our church.

I called Bruce and blurted out everything. He said, "Meet me at the hospital and we'll pray. We hung up and I breathed a simple prayer, "God help us. Keep him alive." Then I was out the door.

Critical Time

After arriving at Citrus Memorial Hospital, I made my way to the front desk. "Where did they take my husband? He had a stroke."

"He's in the emergency room. Go on back, hon," one of the nurses told me. However, before I could leave, I was confronted by a grumpy foreign doctor who said, "He had a stroke because he wouldn't take blood thinners." *I don't need that kind of negativity right now.* Not coming up with a response, I stared at him. *What an insensitive idiot.* I walked on.

My heart sank as I rounded the corner into Ron's cubby. Hooked up to several beeping machines, he looked so sick and helpless, and I couldn't do a thing. Except pray.

The first few hours are critical with a stroke. Coincidentally, or perhaps not, I'd recently read up on a clot-busting drug that needs to be given within about three hours after a stroke to be effective. Thrombolytic medications are approved for the immediate treatment of stroke and heart attack, and the most commonly used drug is **tissue plasminogen activator (tPA)**.

Two hours passed when I asked the doctor, "Did you give him the clot buster?" He said, "We don't want to give him the tPA because if there's a mass in his brain, the medicine could kill him. If it's a clot, it would break it up, but we can't be sure without an MRI." Time was tick, tick, ticking away.

Finally, he got an MRI, but they said they couldn't treat him. Our dinky hospital didn't have a neurology faculty and he'd have to be airlifted to Shands in

Gainesville. This would be the destination where they could treat someone with his condition.

Pastor Bruce soon arrived. Ron was really animated and tried to talk with him, but his talk was babble and made no sense. I locked eyes with Bruce and forced a smile. He suggested we head out to the waiting room, where he prayed, beseeching God on our behalf. Relieved, I felt some peace God had us both in his capable hands.

After Bruce left, I headed back to Ron's room before he was to leave on the helicopter ride. He was quiet with his eyes closed, but they'd suddenly pop open. Then he'd say, "That is really weird," over and over again, and repeating, "What was your want?" Everything had the word "want" in it. Last, but not least, he shared, "I feel like I'm here, but not here."

At this point, I wasn't sure if he was hovering between life and death. In order to remain calm and make sense of what he could be experiencing, I began questioning him.

I asked, "Are you floating up above your body?"

"Yes," he said. "I see all of you, and I'm watching over it all."

"Are you walking through a tunnel toward a bright light?"

"Yes," he said. I see everyone I've ever known in my life. Everything I ever did. "

The questions ended when a group of six men and women rushed into the room, rolled him onto a large piece of canvas, and transferred him onto a gurney and out the door.

Before being whisked away to the ambulance, he called for Andrew—his first son.

What does this mean, Lord? Is he going home now to be with you? I steeled myself for the next part of this journey—whatever it may be.

Storm Clouds

I left the hospital, winds whipping at my face. Temperatures had plunged, and steely gray clouds rolled in. *Dress warmly before Gainesville.* I started making my mental checklist as I drove home. *Get gas.* Before arriving at the station, two guys in a big truck pulled up beside me, waving and honking. *Now what?* They mouthed and pointed, "You got water shooting out the bottom of your car!"

Great. Directly in front of the station, I pulled in as steam rolled out from under the hood. Fumbling for the latch, I raised it and stared at a jumbled mess of wires and hoses. Sighing, I breathed a short prayer. *Help me, Lord!* Car troubles were out of my league. *I wish someone would tell me what to do.* At that moment, a man walked by, saw my distress, and took pity on me. Using a bunch of towels, he pulled up a dangling black hose and said, "See this here? This clamp is missing from your radiator hose. It's blown off and all the water leaked out."

Like moths to a flame, car troubles attract more mechanics and wanna-bes, as another man soon joined in. Working together, they quickly clamped on the hose, so I thanked them and prayed my way home. I believe God's angels led me there with no further trouble.

I pulled into the driveway, shut off the car, got out and locked the door. A burning smell assaulted my nostrils, so I sniffed at a crack in the hood. Transmission fluid also had leaked out on the driveway. *Great.* This was the least of my problems.

My jaw dropped surveying the scene before me. Thirty minutes prior, I'd left the hospital where my husband was being airlifted to another city. Still in the dark about his condition, my mind raced. Was he going to live or die? Would he be able to walk or would he be paralyzed? Would he become a tube-fed vegetable? *Am I now totally alone?* Wobbly, and held up only by my leaking, patched-together car, I faced another problem demanding my attention.

It was as if God's hand (or something else perhaps) had scooped up our big tent in the middle of the yard and flipped it. The tent was like a dog lying on its back, with its legs (support poles) sticking straight up in the air. Our beautiful blue Plumbago bushes were crushed under its weight. Our front yard in complete shambles.

Another smaller tent from the driveway was twisted, mangled, and completely destroyed. It was possible a tornado blew through during my short time at the hospital, and our yard turned into a war zone. I know now, it's true during a disaster a person's body is traumatized. People react in a variety of ways such as screaming or crying. Others begin the task of recovery. I'd never in my life encountered such trauma in such a short period of time. What would I do?

God what are you doing here? I don't understand. Overwhelmed and numb, this new turn of events was almost unbearable, and I still had to figure out how to get to Shands hospital—an hour and a half drive from home.

In the driveway was a knocked-over plastic shelf holding some promotional ink pens. Now, as a sea of scattered blue pens covered the driveway, it was time to being the process of recovery. Although my heart and mind was as shattered as our yard, I slowly, methodically, picked up them up—one by one.

"Through the Lord's mercies we are not consumed, because His compassions fail not. They are new every morning, and His faithfulness is great."

Lamentations 3:22-23

Yard Work

My thoughts were going in a million different directions. *God, what am I to do? I must get to the hospital. The car won't make it. The yard needs cleaned up.* Who can I call to help? *Please show me.*

My first thought was to again call the youth pastor and tell him I needed help, thinking he'd send the entire youth group—perhaps as a mission project. I called Bruce and he did send help—but not like I thought.

There are certain people you know you can call in any situation and they'll be there. Three boys showed up—Jonathan, David, and Josh—my first angels. These brothers were members of our Sunday school class and part of a sweet family of five. They knew how to serve others. For instance, when there were fund raising banquets for charity causes, we'd sit while they served food the entire night. They'd collect money for wreaths to lay on tombs of military veterans at Bushnell National Cemetery. There was nothing they wouldn't do to help.

Probably within the hour, things were straightened up, then on to the next problem. I rode with the boys back to Citrus Memorial to find out if Ron had actually been airlifted. They dropped me off and I checked in. He'd been airlifted to Shands Hospital at approximately five p.m. Yes, he was flying above us in a helicopter, but there was another trip he would take much further than a few miles down the road.

Good Friends

From the hospital lobby, I briefly rested and peered out the window into the dark, rain-slicked parking lot, gazing upon hospital lights reflecting in the puddles. I was alone, but didn't feel alone. I knew God had brought me this far, and wouldn't let me go. He was about to send the second set of angels to care for me.

Ron and Jackie. Their names flashed before me just as the hospital sign did moments before.

Another generous retired couple from our Sunday school class, they were active in a ministry called the Agape House, which helps single mothers in need of clothes, food, and a compassionate ear. Jackie was director of this non-profit, and Ron helped out before he passed away in 2018.

I phoned Jackie and told her of my dilemma. At this point, it was getting on six o'clock. She said, "Sit tight. We'll be right over and get you to Gainesville." I knew they had a thirty minute drive from their home, then another hour and a half to arrive at Shands. *Thank you, God, for these generous people who gave up their quiet evening at home to take care of me.*

Once they arrived, we all headed into the darkness for the long trip. How can you thank someone for just dropping everything to come to your aid? They truly were my angels and I thanked them over and over. They said they were happy to help and I knew they meant every word.

Shands' Brain Ward

Around eleven p.m., we finally reached Gainesville and University of Florida Shands Hospital. Streets were dark and free of bustling traffic. The work day was long over. People had finished shopping, and returned home to eat dinner and settle in for the night. Signs whipped in the wind, with trees and roads glistening from the rain. Stoplights blinked yellow, reflecting in the rain-soaked road. I squeezed my eyes tightly shut; hoping I'd wake and all would have been a dream.

Construction surrounded us, and we had no idea where to go. My first instinct was head for the main building, so we parked in the garage and walked a country mile through boarded up walkways. Cold night air stung our faces as we forged our way to the entrance.

The main lobby opened up into a different world. Like bugs coming out of the walls, people spilled out from everywhere—large groups, wheelchairs, sick people, and well people. Illness never sleeps. Dazed, I shuffled my way to the big desk marked "information." A helpful-looking elderly woman sat behind the desk and smiled. "May I help you?"

"Yes, I hope so. My husband was airlifted here to your hospital. Could you tell me where he is?" I assumed he would already have been taken to a room. Actually, he was still in emergency waiting for a room to open up in the neurology ward.

Bone tired, I forced one leg in front of the other. I'd been going nonstop since 11:30 that morning, with Ron's status still unknown, and twelve hours later, I'd need to stay awake much longer. I managed to find emergency, and was directed to a large room off to the side.

As I mentioned earlier, Ron is a very large man. Beds in emergency were probably about five feet, seven inches long, and the first thing I noticed was the bottom half of his legs hanging off the end of the bed. He looked extremely uncomfortable. He saw me, brightened, and babbled incoherently again. He begged to go home. I said, "Honey, that's impossible. You've just had a stroke and they have to take care of you." He gave me a blank stare and repeated his begging.

His doctor was a tiny, Asian woman who'd seen Ron earlier, but couldn't converse with him. This was extremely frustrating to him, as I knew it was for her. Once she returned, I began the long journey of being his interpreter—something I continue to this day. Since she couldn't understand Ron, she spoke directly to me— virtually ignoring him. Rapid firing questions, she asked, "When did the stroke occur? How quickly did he get to the hospital? What did they give him? What did he say?" As we talked, Ron's jaw clenched and his eyes narrowed.

Grimly, she said, "Ron had a massive stroke on the right side of his brain, and some bleeding. He also had two smaller strokes on the left side. The left side of the brain is where our language resides. He's able to talk, but when he speaks, the words don't make sense." She said he'd be transferred to a room in the neurology ward hopefully within the next hour.

Finally, two men arrived at three a.m., and snatched his gurney. They fast walked as I sprinted to keep up, my legs somehow moving, but the rest of my body in a fog. From emergency we wheeled through a glass walkway over the street, onto elevators, several different floors, and then arrived at what appeared to be an oasis in the desert compared to the frantic emergency room. The neurology ward was so quiet you could hear a pin drop, and there was one nurse per patient.

A man almost as big as Ron entered the room and greeted us. Gary, tall and gregarious, was to be Ron's nurse and exuded warmth and friendliness that made us feel right at home. I wanted to cry and crumple into a heap. Exhaustion was taking over after being awake for a day and a half. The parade of nurses, technicians, and doctors began, and Ron was hooked up to all manner of machines, beeping, beeping, blipping. The night wasn't over, so I settled in for the long haul.

Although barely coherent, he was prodded, poked, analyzed, and hooked up for an EEG. The technician appeared with a marker and began drawing little dots all over his head. An electroencephalogram (**EEG**) is a test that detects electrical activity in your brain using small, flat metal discs (electrodes) attached to your scalp. Your brain cells communicate via electrical impulses and are active constantly, even when asleep. After mapping out Ron's scalp, he then used a gel to attach little wires all over his head. As he worked, he said to Ron, "You have a very regal head," which made me smile, but produced no response from Ron. He then wound a large gauze bandage around Ron's head until he appeared as if he'd been in a car crash with a severe head injury. Once he finished, the wires poking out of his head looked like little alfalfa sprouts. I caught myself laughing again and feeling a little lighter. The machine took over—now reading and beeping his brain activity and giving doctors readouts inside his skull.

They did another test called an Echocardiogram (Echo). This is a type of ultrasound test that uses high-pitched sound waves sent through a device called a transducer. The device picks up echoes of sound waves as they bounce off different parts of your heart. I observed pictures of Ron's beating heart, and could even hear it! They did a color contrast to inspect it more closely. At times, the picture looked like a little dancing man, and sometimes a face.

Soon, a nurse arrived to give him a sponge bath. She and Gary sponged him down from head to toe, and it was a beautiful scene to witness the care this lovely woman took in cleaning his face, neck, arms, legs, and stomach. He groaned with ecstasy, but would have been mortified had he been aware of what was really happening. Being privy to this special time brought to mind the loving way Jesus washed the feet of each of his twelve disciples, demonstrating how much our heavenly Father loves us. God sent this angel nurse to lovingly wash away the stress of the stroke. Knowing he was in good hands, I slumped into the slippery recliner, and dozed off.

The next day began the doctor parade. Like the Pied Piper, fresh-faced young pups in white coats tagged behind and hung onto their master's every word. The attending physician tooted, they tooted, he spoke, and they spoke. Hungering for knowledge, they were learning, observing, questioning. Ron was the specimen in this little play, the rat in the cage, the cells under a microscope. This is how they looked at him—at first.

As serious faces focused intently on this nameless person in bed, they were blank and unflinching until Ron perked up, eyes wide open, and said, "What is your want?" He repeated this again and again. Men and women of all nationalities were represented, and a young doctor-in-waiting finally cracked a smile. He looked around to see if anyone else was smiling. They weren't, but I believe this was a defining moment for this young man.

I believe he saw a man, personality in full bloom, sitting up perky, alert and talking. Even if Ron didn't make a lick of sense, this was a human being with a life he was living before his body betrayed him. This body was a man under a microscope, but he had wants, needs, and feelings just as they did.

Even after a stroke, he's still able to make people laugh—like he did before.

This young doctor smiled through the rest of the entire briefing, then the young pups were gone. The attending doctor remained afterward with some serious news. I had to make some quick decisions.

War Room

The doctor shared with me how serious Ron's condition was, and how he could stroke again. He asked for permission to give Ron a dose of super blood thinner, which he said may or may not work. I needed time to pray, so I took the elevator down to Shands' chapel and sat in the front row, alone. The chapel was cool and quiet and I pleaded with God, "Please don't take my husband. Please let him live!" I cried until all tears dried up.

God, what are you doing? I don't understand. We were doing exactly what we thought you wanted. We thought we'd clearly heard from you to sell off everything and move to South America. Maybe do some mission work.

I felt backed up against the wall, and needed to burn off nervous energy. After leaving the chapel, I wore a path throughout Shands' hallways back and forth, repeating, "I go to the rock that is higher than I," not even knowing what verse it was from. The words formed in my mind and as I repeated them, they seared a truth into my soul. A truth there was someone in charge—much bigger than me.

Later at home, I looked it up in the Bible.

"Hear my cry, O God;

Attend to my prayer.

From the end of the earth I will cry to You,

When my heart is overwhelmed;

Lead me to the rock that is higher than I.

For You have been a shelter for me,

A strong tower from the enemy."

Psalm 61:1-3 (NKJV)

After prayers, our circumstances were about to take an unexpected turn.

Day Seven

Day seven was moving day. The 10th floor had a completely different atmosphere. Leaving behind peace and quiet of the blue neurology ward threw me off balance, as we were plunged into chaos inside a cheery yellow room—complete with a roommate—and more. When we arrived, this man obviously had a big family with visitors lining the walls. The cramped room had one straight back chair, which I grabbed and positioned against the window, silently praying thanks for the reclining one I had left behind. Small blessings.

The previous night had been difficult. Ron became agitated several times, yelling and trying to get out of bed. I tried to calm him by saying, "Honey, you don't need to go to the bathroom, you have a catheter." He'd lift the covers, say "Ohhhhh," and put them back down. He'd be still for a moment before the process repeated.

Prior to the agitation, he'd rub his head, followed by his legs violently shaking and feet slamming against the bed frame. I was scared, but didn't send for the nurse. They monitored his vitals and if anything was terribly wrong, they'd be there in two shakes. When the nurse returned, I shared what had happened, but she didn't seem concerned.

Now, staring out the window of our new room, I struggled to ignore the visitors and imagine normal life going on outside of these four walls. Sunlight spilled inside and warmed my face as I gazed into a beautiful sunrise and people going about their day. A tall building numbered 1515 on the front sat across the street, probably full of busy workers getting lots of important things accomplished. Swaying palm trees lining the street seemed to mock me. Bone tired, my thoughts drifted to the upcoming night and attempting to sleep in this upright position. Just another day in paradise.

Meanwhile, Ron was upright and awake. His nurse checked vitals, and a nutritionist jotted down his order for lunch and breakfast. It turned out this wasn't necessary. Within the hour, the flurry of activity ceased, and another visitor appeared.

Lisa was a Shands' Rehab nurse with such a sweet disposition; I knew she had to be another heaven-sent angel. After introductions, she handed me a brochure and said, "Ron's coming along well, and he's ready to leave the hospital for rehab." I stared at pictures of a beautiful building surrounded by trees and flowers, reminding me of a resort.

She continued, "UF Health Shands Rehab Hospital has 40 beds specifically for patients who have suffered strokes, traumatic brain and spinal cord injuries, amputations, burns or major joint replacements."

The idea of a change of scenery was exciting—and welcome. However, not wanting to get my hopes up, I decided to be honest with her and said, "This looks wonderful, but we can't afford this. We have no insurance, and no money for rehab." Dollar signs piled up in my head, with a bill well into six figures.

She smiled. "Don't worry about the cost. Shands sets aside several charity beds, and he qualifies. This is completely free to you, and this rehab is one of the best facilities in Florida. He'll receive the best care possible, with his own private room and three meals a day. There's also daily speech, occupational and physical therapy." She stopped for a moment and touched my arm. "And just so you know, this usually doesn't happen this fast.

It's a blessing because other people were on the list in front of him, but they're not physically ready. His name was actually pretty far down, but he's the only one ready to go."

My eyes grew wide. "Wow…really?" I exhaled stress and despair from the past week, and hope rose. Amazed at how God was working, I tried not to get too excited—yet. I swiped at tears that had streaked my cheeks. "How soon do we leave?" I asked.

"There's a bed ready for him right now," she said. "If you agree and sign the forms, we'll get him ready and transport him by ambulance. You can ride alongside him." She gave me a comforting smile and hug. I nearly burst into tears again. "We'll see you down there in a bit. Oh, and I want you to know that you'll *both* be taken care of." I nodded with relief.

A glimmer of God's goodness.

Miracle Walk

Ron was released from the hospital and wheeled down to a waiting van. We took the short ride to rehab, which consisted of hopping on the freeway and getting off at the next exit.

At Shands Rehab, the attendant pushed Ron's wheelchair into a spacious lobby, but once he stopped pushing, Ron rose and walked on his own. A whirl of activity followed as they took his name and personal info. Quickly, he was ushered to a room.

Ron's nurse was a beautiful African-American woman named Kay. She jotted some things on a chart, and asked him, "Would you like something to eat?"

Smiling, he replied, "What is your want?"

Again, I could see he didn't understand her question, so I jumped in and said, "Yes, he would."

Ron's words were a mess, but he was still his normal, outgoing self—for the most part. He was flirty with Kay, and overjoyed to be out of the hospital. I wasn't sure at that point if I'd even be allowed to stay with him. I explained our lack of car situation.

She said, "Honey, don't you worry about a thing. We'll work something out so you can stay with him."

Shortly, a delicious-looking meal of fried chicken, potatoes and green beans was delivered to the room, the smells reaching my nostrils and making my mouth water. Hunger pangs stabbed like never before, and like a ravenous wolf, I eyed his plate. Very little sleep paired with an empty stomach, and I was a walking zombie.

I must have been a pitiful sight because another nurse came in to check on him—but instead took pity on me. She asked, "How about you, hon, are you hungry? Have you had anything to eat today?" I shook my head, fighting back tears again. Like a mother hen, she reassured me. "Now he's the patient, but you also need to take care of yourself. I'm going to give you a voucher for the cafeteria. Don't hesitate to get whatever you want. Even dessert, okay?"

I nodded and my eyes glazed over as I pictured heaping plates full of food. Snapping out my food dream, I said, "Oh, I will, believe me—after fried chicken and potatoes."

She patted my back. "Let's take a little walk. He'll be okay for a bit."

We chatted and walked pristine, waxed floors through mazes of hallways and around many corners before finally arriving at the cafeteria. After a week of unknowns about Ron's condition, this conversation and mealtime made me feel normal. I loaded up my plate with chicken, potatoes, green beans, and brownie bites for dessert. Food never tasted so good—I'd not realized how emotionally and physically starved I was. Rehab offered a chance to rest, relax, and eat my first hot meal in a week. God's mercies are new every morning.

Later, Kay returned after we'd eaten and all the trays were picked up. That's when she told me a shocking truth. "I've been with Shands Rehab for seven years," she said, "and in that entire time I've *never* seen a stroke patient walk in that front door on their own. Ron is a first."

"Really?" I murmured, contemplating her words. "A miracle."

"Yes, it really is." She shook her head, "What he did is amazing. Without fail, stroke patients are always brought in on a stretcher. He's a walking, talking miracle."

The news was like honey to my ears. To hear that after having three strokes, Ron was doing things no one else had done before him, I anticipated a full recovery— even though his words were still mostly jumbled.

Kay said, "Also, he'll be moving to a room down the hall. It's a private room, and you'll be able to sleep on a mattress beside his bed on the floor. Make sure to get some rest tonight, because tomorrow he'll be starting his rehab schedule. It'll be difficult and draining for him, so you rest up, too, hon. He'll need support."

"Okay, thanks for everything, Kay," I said. Even a mattress on the floor sounded like heaven.

Room 1923 was now our home for the next seven days. Throughout the night, nurses and attendants swirled in and out, taking his vitals and giving him pills. Despite all that, I crashed into a very deep, dreamless sleep.

It's Still Me

After a fairly good night's sleep, the nurse roused us the next morning before 7:00 a.m., with pills and nudges to get to breakfast by 7:30. She warned that Ron's day ahead would be full—and difficult.

We dressed and headed to the bustling dining room, spotting two open chairs at one of the long tables. Many men and women were here recovering from major life illnesses. Patiently, we waited as they passed out covered breakfast trays full of food. Ron's appetite hadn't changed much. He dug in and cleaned his plate.

Therapy began immediately following breakfast. First, was a visit to the office of his speech therapist. We settled in, and after introductions her tone became serious. She explained, "Since the stroke you've experienced, you've been left with Wernicke's Aphasia. Have you heard of it?" She looked intently at him, then at me.

I picked up on her verbal cues, knowing I was now the one in charge. I shook my head. "Not really—what is it—exactly?"

She played a touching video, called "Heart to Heart," and we all fixated on the computer screen. The tears flowed, as my chest ached and I felt the crushing weight of all we had lost.

Up to that point, I'd been keeping it together. A funny illustration is the movie, *Bowfinger,* starring Steve Martin. Eddie Murphy plays a very pampered actor by the name of Kit. He has everything in the world a person could want, except a very tentative grip on reality. He constantly runs to his therapist at *Mindhead,* just so this guy can give him three little words. "Keep it Together."

He'll ask Eddie, "What is your name?" And Eddie Murphy will reply with "Kit. K-I-T, Keep It Together. My name is K-I-T. Keep it together. Keep it together. Keep it together." He repeats this over and over, trying to pull himself back from the brink of losing it.

That's exactly what I'd been doing as I cared for Ron after his stroke. I was K-I-T-ing it. But now, a moment of concern from someone I didn't even know, I was L-O-S-I-N-G it. I needed to release all the emotions that had been building for the past week. I still didn't know what we were going to do after rehab was over, but at that moment, I wasn't concerned. I needed a good cry and the shoulder sitting at the desk across from me was the closest thing I'd had since the week before.

As we sat side by side now in the speech therapist's office, Ron's face was blank with confusion, which was our new normal. An aphasia patient will have trouble expressing what's in their mind. Even if they're thinking the right words, the words coming out of their mouth are completely different. He still spoke mostly gibberish.

After our little talk with the speech therapist, he was exhausted. She said, "When there's a brain injury, exercising the brain will be more exhausting to the patient than actually exercising the body." Surprised, I tucked away this bit of information for the future. She said in order to talk with him; I'd have to use very few words. Actually, I'd become very skilled at reducing a sentence down to its simplest form.

Next, it was time to go to physical therapy (PT). He's always been very strong and able to handle physical labor with no problem. However, strength is usually the first to go after a stroke. The therapist and I were not prepared for what we were about to see.

For PT, there's one giant room with floor mats on a raised platform, along with weights, bikes, and elastic bands. It looked like a regular small gym, but everyone was there for one purpose—regain strength they had lost. Our physical therapist had Ron practice little things that were no problem for him, such as squeezing a ball, lifting a weight, or pedaling a bike. He was bored, and she saw the need to up the game.

She glanced at me then said, "Ron, we're going for a walk." Energized, he darted out in front as we struggled to keep up. Nervously, I braced for his fall as he scooted over rocks in the road. However, he did just fine, and we circled around the outside of the building, with him in the lead.

The therapist laughed and said, "He certainly has no problem with strength. Actually, I've been here 25 years and have never seen anyone have so much energy after a stroke."

I laughed. "Yep, that's Ron. Like Hercules—lots of strength and energy, which probably helped him through this. His main issue right now is speech. That's going to be a challenge." She nodded. Ron made a beeline for the door as we walked behind and chatted. It was nice to have another woman to talk with, and I enjoyed her company.

During the night, when Ron was sleeping, my thoughts drifted back to the hospital. Just a few days prior, my bed for that week was a hard chair. I had no change of clothes and no shower. Meals were sparse since I didn't have extra money to buy them. Sometimes I'd roll up my sweats, walk down the hall and into the little kitchen meant for medical interns and families, and heat a cup of broth or hot chocolate just to put something into my stomach.

After seven days in the hospital, rehab was a vacation. It gave us a bit of rest, and glimmer of hope perhaps Ron was on the upswing and well enough to come home soon. He was being taken care of in the best possible way through physical, occupational, and speech therapy, and I was not alone in desiring him to get better. Now I had a team working hand in hand with us, gently pushing him back to a normal life. Little did I know, how long the road would be to recovery, but for now, I was grateful for the care I received alongside him. Again, our own personal team of angels. I truly felt God's presence and provision.

The hospital stay was seven days. Rehab was also exactly seven days. The significance of the number seven was not lost on me.

Rehab Celebrity

One night, my growling tummy sent me to the cafeteria in search of a snack. The large room, usually bustling with patients, doctors, and nurses was empty at that late hour, since most exhausted patients were tucked into bed. As I rounded the corner, I was surprised to see someone sitting alone. A fashionable, elderly gentleman in a wheelchair, he wore a brown fedora and thick, colorful scarf around his neck. A blanket covered his lap. As I approached, his entire face broke into a warm and welcoming smile, so I sat next to him.

We shook hands and I introduced myself. "Hello, my name is Penelope."

His eyes twinkled, with the smile never leaving his face. "Very nice to meet you, Penelope. My name is Ellis."

He said, "Penelope. What a lovely name. You know, I've noticed you at meals. Is that your husband you're with?"

Sighing, I said, "Yes. He had a stroke and spent seven days in the hospital. He's very upset about being here and doesn't want to stay. I hate to admit this, but I'm really tiring of all the griping and complaining. I had to get away from him or I'll say something I'll regret."

He said, "Penelope, you're a good wife and a great helpmate to him. He's very blessed to have you by his side. I can see how much you care. Many people here don't have anyone. But you must remember to care for yourself or you won't have anything left for him. You must take time to refresh and renew. It's fine to get away by yourself. Don't deny yourself that time."

I blinked away tears, as his kind words soaked into my soul. I didn't know what the future held once we left for home, but I did know everything from finances—to Ron's care—was squarely on my shoulders. However, for this moment, my heart was touched by our encounter, another small blessing sent from above. God surely sent me into the cafeteria to be able to share with this wonderful and charming man.

I asked, "What happened that brought you to rehab, Ellis?"

"I had a stroke, too. That's why I'm in the wheelchair," he said.

"Are you married?" I asked.

"I was, a long time ago, but we got divorced. I wasn't a very nice man back then."

Smiling, I shook my head. "That's hard to believe. You're so encouraging and easy to talk with."

"I hope so. I'm a book editor and author, and many years ago traveled in circles with the rich and famous. I drank. I partied. A lot. I'm an alcoholic, but I've been sober now for a long time."

"What happened to turn your life around, Ellis?"

He said, "I put my faith and trust in God and become a Christian, and that was the end of my partying lifestyle. I'm at peace now. His face truly radiated inner joy and love for others. I felt as if I'd met a kindred spirit.

"Hmmm," I said, "That's funny you being a book editor, as I'm currently writing a romance novel, and just feel stuck. I was pushing hard to complete the book the exact day Ron had a stroke. I'm not sure I'll ever finish now, and sometimes think maybe I should just give it up and stop writing altogether."

Ellis said, "No. No. Penelope, you keep on writing. Finish that book. All things will work out as they should."

During the time in rehab, I was without a computer and no way to search for him. Little did I know what an amazing person my new friend was.

Who was this Ellis?

Ellis Amburn was a 1954 graduate of Texas Christian University. He worked as a reporter for Newsweek before going into the book publishing industry where he rose to the position of editor, working for such well-known publishers as Delacorte Press, Coward-McCann, and William Morrow. During his career, Amburn was an editor for authors such John le Carré, Belva Plain, Muriel Spark, Joshua Logan and for Jack Kerouac, who would be the subject of Amburn's 1998 book on which Leonardo DiCaprio has optioned film rights.

Amburn served as editorial director for G. P. Putnam's Sons and in addition worked as a ghostwriter for Priscilla Presley, Shelley Winters, Peggy Lee and Zsa Zsa Gabor. In 1990, he produced his first biography on fellow Texan Roy Orbison that led to further such books. He's noted for his exhaustive research, even going so far as to live for several weeks at the home of the parents of Orbison's first wife, Claudette Frady-Orbison. His books have generated controversy at times (such as his biography of Janis Joplin), and he is reviled by many Orbison fans for presenting hearsay as fact.

Having no idea of this celebrity in the midst of rehab, I got a clue when one night a group of dewy-eyed college students came to visit and sit at his feet. From a distance, I watched them hang on his every word, and there would be periods of silence—then bursts of laughter.

He gave me enough information so when I arrived home, I searched out his work. As I poured over his bio, I was amazed and knew for sure we never would have met had I not been in rehab at that exact moment.

Ellis was like an old friend who listened, encouraged, and comforted when he was the one who needed comfort. Sometimes it only takes one small touch to bring about an extraordinary change in someone's life. He radiated a light that lives on in my heart.

Meeting Ellis was a small part of one of many ExtraOrdinary Detours. Ellis moved inside circles of the rich and famous. He wrote books about them. He partied hard like them. Until he had an extraordinary encounter with God. He found God, and I found Ellis in rehab. Ellis was wise and kind and brought a ray of sunshine into my frazzled existence. I will never forget him.

He died August 18, 2018, after a long illness.

Ellis Amburn. (2021, July 10). Retrieved September 14, 2021, from Wikipedia website: https://en.wikipedia.org/wiki/Ellis_Amburn

Lost at Home

By the time we received word from the doctors about Ron's release, I was more than ready. Honestly, I wearied of hearing continual complaints about how tired he was, and how he wanted to go home. I was, too, but had no one to complain to. *God, you've got to give me strength. I don't know how I'm going to handle all this at home.*

Most people don't realize how your life can change in an instant and rock your world. I've learned to appreciate the life we have—even if it isn't perfect. Which it never is. Before Ron was taken to the hospital, he was a man—and my equal. But when I brought him home on Tuesday, November 26, he was like a little child again. I was now the adult in charge, and his teacher, too.

Before his stroke, I found myself becoming increasingly irritated with him at times, so I prayed. *God, help me love Ron like you do.* Once back home, I pondered that perhaps God allowed this stroke to help me love him unconditionally. The thought of my praying this prayer—may have caused his stroke—made me absolutely sick. I know God doesn't bring trouble upon us, but He does allow things in our lives to bring us to the point he wants us to be. Now I wondered…*Were all the plans we made: sell out everything, get passports, move to Ecuador, and do mission work; were they God's plans? I don't think so.* His plans are greater than ours. Higher than ours.

Once back home, the first few days were especially rough.

Day one he woke and was confused at his surroundings. Walking from room to room, he'd open up all the doors and closets, and say, "I feel like I lost all of it." Then repeat the same questions: "What happened to me, how long have we lived here, and what happened to my mom and dad?"

First, I'd deeply inhale, then for what seemed like an endless loop, slowly retell the story. Actually, I thought about recording the entire conversation and just pushing the "play" button each time. Date of the stroke? November 13. How many days was he in the hospital and rehab? 14. What happened to me? Stroke.

Becoming upset with him didn't help. If I let irritation show or raise my voice to him, he'd cry. If I lost my cool we both paid the price. I was the buffer between him and the world by staying calm and filtering everything he saw and heard. If we watched a television show with any kind of violence, it upset him. So that was out, too.

Day two was a blur, as he kept me running after him like crazy. After breakfast, I planned to catch up on laundry when he decided to go for a walk. I had visions of him becoming lost in the neighborhood, never finding his way home, and having to call out police and sniffing dogs. In order to avert another crisis I tagged down our street after him, struggling to catch up. November was cold, and I shivered in my flip flops and no coat (after all, we live in Florida).

Shortly after walking, we returned home and slowly began cleaning up yard sale items in the driveway. We pulled clothes off tables, brought them inside, and hung wet blankets to dry. We made space on a shelf and two tables where Ron could sort his tools. Some items were shoved into the garage, and some tossed to the curb for free pickup. Our driveway was now as neat as a pin. The stuff under the tarp in the front yard still had to be tackled—the same tarp that was once a tent before the storm blew through and bent the poles. I mused how funny that a person's life can appear normal—even if far from it.

On the positive side, God allowed for some amusing moments along the way. Although not so funny at the time, they allowed us to breathe a bit easier. One such moment involved our gray Burmese cat named Pepper. I wasn't sure she'd return, because I'd left in such a rush, completely forgetting about her, and she had to find her own food for two weeks. One morning, she showed up, putting her little paws up on the glass doors. What a blessing to see her again!

Ron put out her food and doused it with water. I said, "Honey, this kind of cat food doesn't need water." His eyes grew wide as he raised his eyebrows in question. Apparently, his brain brought up the memory of Kibbles 'N Bits, a cat food making its own gravy.

Another night after we'd finished eating pizza, he yelped from the bathroom. I raced frantically down the hall, imagining the worst. "We've got a problem here," he said, pointing to his lips and nose. "Blood is coming out of my pores!"

Stifling a laugh, my eyes lifting heavenward, I said, "Honey, that red is a smudge of pizza sauce." I wiped it off and we hugged and laughed while looking at our reflections in the mirror. Crisis averted.

Ron pushed himself a little more each day. He studied store ads continually, and would say, "That's a super deal," or "that's a rip off." One day, we drove to Circle K to buy a couple of newspapers. As we drove home, he got excited and yelled, "Turn left, turn left!

We're gonna get some chicken!" The way he said the word CHICK-in! tickled my funny bone, and I couldn't stop laughing. He was bound determined to get that CHICK-in.

Instinctively, I knew what he wanted, and that was to drive into Save-a-lot, so we headed that way. Yes, chicken was on sale for $1.59/pound, and after picking up a few other items, those two papers turned into $25.00.

Light moments aside, others were not so funny, and I'd have to turn away. My heart would break as he'd read the same newspaper page all day. I purchased a paper so he'd know what was going on in the world; having no idea he'd have to learn how to read all over again.

Trying to be as hands off as possible, I gave him space to relearn what he needed to know. For instance, allowing him to cook an egg like he did in rehab. It was fried and a turned out a bit overcooked, but was edible. He made chocolate chip cookies—without flour—so they were pretty flat. Despite this, I ate them with gusto, since anything with chocolate is fantastic.

For the times I sensed he still needed guidance, I'd patiently try to walk him through the steps. We did everything together, and that brought us closer. My irritation eased up, allowing him room to feel accomplishment. Even though his attempts took two times longer, it was all worthwhile.

Some days seemed completely normal, and then some were whack-a-doodle. Just know that no matter what you're going through, you'll survive and tomorrow is a brand new day. I experienced a light-hearted feeling on

November 29, when he didn't wake up confused, walking room to room, or peering into closets.

Things had calmed down a bit, but at this point, I still thought in terms of worst case scenarios. Minute by minute, I prayed desperate prayers, assuring myself God knew about our situation and had us in his grip. This assurance was enough to keep me going yet another day.

"Do not let your hearts be troubled. Trust in God; trust also in me."

John 14:1 (NLT)

Black Book

Soon, another dilemma presented itself. Ron literally was like a child again, and couldn't remember simple things most of us take for granted—things like the alphabet, numbers, days of the week or months. Once we learned these in school, they're tucked away forever, and we don't give a second thought as to how our computer brains work on autopilot. We live and communicate daily without much effort. Words and numbers are there, and just come to mind when the need arises.

Now, two weeks after a lightning strike to his brain, Ron didn't know how to ask for what he wanted. He didn't even know his own name—or mine.

Speech therapy was out of the question. We didn't have the money to pay for it, so I knew I'd now become his teacher. It's sometimes difficult to converse with another adult on the same level, but if you have one who doesn't understand the simplest of things; it's near impossible.

I prayed about this night and day. Unsure of exactly where to begin, we began at square one. I prepared as if teaching a child in kindergarten, and then we'd progress from there. With this in mind, I rolled up my sleeves and devised a plan.

First, I headed to the dollar store to purchase a three-pack of miniature, marbleized notebooks. He desperately needed a notebook he could keep ready in his pocket. His little black book.

Next, I imagined back to kindergarten, where our teachers established a firm foundation on which to build.

We learned the basics. I knew that's where we needed to start, and it would take quite a while to return to where he was prior to the stroke—if that ever happened.

So each day began with an acute sense of purpose. Our daily lessons consisted of ABC's and 123's, colors, months of the year, days of the weeks, seasons, and holidays. I'd write the lessons on a big white board, and then straight into his little black book. He learned letters and numbers and then repeated them back to me.

We both grew up in the baby boomer generation, and learned to read using phonetics. For each vowel, I'd make the sound that went along with it. A, E, I, O, U and sometimes Y. Short sounds, such as, Ah, Eh, Ih, Awe, Uh, and long sounds that had the same sound as the letter name. After that, we'd do the same with the 24 consonants. Buh, Cuh, Duh, Fffff...and on and on. When he had trouble remembering, I'd give him a weak smile and say, "Honey, they're right in front of you inside your trusty book."

At times, I struggled to keep things in perspective, and words from Ron's speech therapist echoed in my mind. She'd said the more progress he makes, the more frustrated he'll become. When he snapped under pressure and communication became a major issue, those words gave me hope—which was daily.

The other major lesson was to relearn his identity. This also went into the book, so the first page listed his name and vital information such as first, middle, last, age, and birth date. I added in his birth place, hometown, and names of his children. All family members' names and birthdays were inserted as well. If I mentioned someone we both knew, their name was written into the book. As we worked, more and more questions arose, and my answers were jotted in.

One day, I got a sinking feeling when discovering he didn't know the names of objects in each room. New lesson. We began in the living room. I made flash cards for couch, lamp, chair, and picture. We covered them over and over. When eating, I'd show, and then tell, writing down names of utensils, plates, napkins, and food. When he brushed his teeth at the end of a long day, it was a perfect opportunity to name toothbrush, toothpaste, toilet, mirror, brush, and shower.

None of this was easy—for him—or me. He'd complain constantly throughout our sessions. Desiring to express himself, he just couldn't get the right word to come out. With aphasia, the person hasn't lost their intelligence, though it seems otherwise. The word he searches for is inside his head, but comes out his mouth a different word—or not at all. The more frustrated he'd become, the less likely he'd be able to express his thoughts. I reminded him we weren't in a race. I'd say, Ron, "Stay calm. Take as much time as you need. Point to something. I'll write it down. Picture it and try to pronounce it." I'd tell him, "Break it into syllables, just like we used to do in elementary school." When it worked, he'd blow out a sigh of relief.

At this point, still, most of the time his words made no sense. Sometimes I could figure them out; sometimes I couldn't. If I wrote it down, he'd usually figure out what I was saying. If he tried to tell me something, he'd have a difficult time expressing it. He repeated himself constantly. I didn't know if he'd ever get back to the way he was before, and my vocabulary was becoming smaller by the day.

Exhausted, I wanted to crawl in bed and never come out again.

I Miss

Do you ever consider how blessed you are? Sometimes, we have no idea until our blessings seem to vanish into thin air. Most of us, myself included, sail through life mostly in a fog, day after day and night after night—thinking things will never change. Family and friends are always at hand, and we take it for granted they'll be close, so we can see their smiles and hear their laughter. Or, we think we can just pick up the phone and they'll be on the other end.

However, this is not so. Life is extremely short. Humans are finite. We're fragile. Things we believe are under our control are not. One day we may wake to find our colorful world has darkened to gray. Blackness sneaks in and steals our joy during the dead of night. All you knew before—is gone.

When tragedy strikes, your world immediately shrinks. Your heart breaks into a million little pieces, and all the concerns you may have had just seconds before such as bills, what to have for lunch, your job, the bank account, that funny looking mole on your back, the disagreement you had with your mom, brother, sister, spouse—gone in an instant. Poof! As if they never existed, the only thing that concerns you right now, in the present moment, is survival.

You hopefully will go into fight mode. Will my loved one live or die? What do I need to do, in my power, to keep him or her alive? God is ultimately in control, but how fast can I make that phone call to 911? Should I keep them awake until emergency arrives? Keep them talking?

You may have a glimmer of concern for yourself, but your focus is mainly on the other person. Why don't we have this concern about our loved ones on a daily, weekly, monthly basis? Why must we wait until we are on the verge of losing them?

There is a time for everything; health AND sickness.

"To everything there is a season, and a time to every purpose under the heaven." Ecclesiastes 3:1 (NKJV)

Sometimes, it's a wake-up call from above.

"So teach us to number our days, that we may apply our hearts unto wisdom." Psalms 90:12 (NKJV)

We should daily soak it all in and breathe "thanks," for the day we've been given. This one wild gift of a life we've been given, full of friends, family, and love. Because you don't know what you've got—until it's gone.

A song comes to mind truly expressing my feelings about our "new normal." The song is "Big Yellow Taxi," by Joni Mitchell, released in 1970. The lyrics lament on how fast things can change around you.

I miss the days of rapid-fire conversation.

I miss not having to stop after each word to explain, write it out, or finger spell.

I miss having someone who is stronger than me.

I miss being the follower instead of the leader.

I miss having someone to collaborate with on decisions.

I miss having someone that can make decisions.

I miss being able to just enjoy the day without thinking about finances, medications, and doctor visits.

I miss carefree days of waking up and planning the next adventure.

I miss feeling like a woman.

I miss feeling happy.

I miss feeling hopeful.

I miss me.

December Depression

December has arrived, and along with it—the depression.

I don't know how to pray anymore. It seems the more I pray, the worse things become. Sometimes, I think about losing myself in a drunken fog and making everything disappear. I know that's not the answer. I'd still wake up every day and now feel a lousy hangover, with mounting bills and pressing paperwork still waiting. I know I must pray for Christ's strength, since I have none left of my own.

A light, cold rain is falling outside at this moment. I sat quietly on the flowered couch where this journey all began, remaining still, just watching and listening. I'm thankful I'm inside and dry, not huddling under a makeshift tent in the woods. *Thank you, Lord, for this shelter.*

Recently, while at the health department, I caught snatches of conversation between a couple sitting behind us. The woman hunched down as if trying to make herself invisible. She said, "I'm hungry," and he replied, "Me, too." How many people are walking around feeling hunger pangs on a daily basis? We live in the richest country in the world, and the poor, hungry and homeless surround us. This stroke thrust us into an entirely new world I've not experienced. I feel humbled and almost invisible myself. We're not homeless, but I feel a kinship with the walking poor.

A few days ago, I needed to run to the post office to mail a package. I could see Ron was completely wiped out, so I told him to rest. He was sprawled out on the bed when I left, and that is where I figured he'd stay. During my trip, I stopped for gas, then to the dollar store to pick up a birthday card for our son, Matt. I ran into a friend, updated her on Ron's situation, and then waited in a long checkout line.

By the time I finished and drove home, Ron was sitting on the porch, crying and scared. He didn't remember our conversation, and said he didn't know where I was. I was shocked how fragile and vulnerable he appeared—like a lost and frightened child. I said, "I'm sorry, honey. Next time I will make sure to leave you a note." Lesson learned.

Christmas Blessings

Christmas day was a simple affair. Usually, Ron decorates the house inside and out, stringing icicle lights across the top, and setting up a manger in the yard. We'd line the driveway with candy canes, drag out the artificial tree from the garage, and spruce it up with ornaments, icicles, and real candy canes. I'm allergic to pine trees, or we'd definitely have one. In Christmases past, he'd assemble whimsical moving ski slopes and train tracks in front of the tree, and would delight in watching the miniature skiers and tiny chugging train.

This year was different. The house was empty of decorations except maybe a snow globe or two, and a couple of presents set aside for our son and his girlfriend. Matt and Rachel came over to stay with us on Christmas afternoon, and gave us a surprising bit of news. They moved their wedding date up from May—to February! We were excited and looked forward to this special event.

That evening, all five of us piled into the car and visited a decked out Christmas display that drew thousands each year. The display was illuminated with about 100,000 lights everywhere! It was so beautiful— like a winter wonderland. Hot chocolate or a mug of cider was also available for purchase. We had a nice time just being together as a family.

This was Christmas, and we had much to celebrate. Ron is alive and I see the future instead of a funeral. I thank God every day for bringing Ron back to me. I know he'll regain a lot of what he lost. With God's help, we both will.

"In everything give thanks; for this is God's will for you in Christ Jesus." 1 Thessalonians 5:18 (NASB)

End of 2013

Another day. Another week. Another year almost over. A year full of sorrows, and I'm not sorry to see it end.

It's been full of broken dreams we were so certain would come to pass. Plans we made as we cleared out, cleaned up and pared down everything we owned. We were so sure of ourselves and God's direction for our lives. Both of us, separately, felt God's strong leading to make these moves. Leading us somewhere. Somewhere unseen, but somewhere, nonetheless. Now, the dreams we had before—were they real or imagined ones? I don't know. My only choice was to throw my hands up in despair (which I am tempted to do), or continue to trust, obey and move forward—perhaps more blindly than ever before.

Maybe that's what God wants from us—to grasp tightly to His hand and trust His leading. Like the layers of an onion, we watch (with anticipation) as the layers of our lives are gently peeled back and our heart's innermost dreams and longings are exposed and fulfilled. They may be dreams we don't even fully realize, or cannot express until God lays them bare for us, and we exclaim, "Oh!" How did you know that was what I wanted when I didn't even know this myself? Then He says, "But, child, I know you better than you know yourself. I knew you before you were even a speck in your mother's womb. I knit you together. I know your entire life. Your beginning and your end." (Romans 8:27, Psalms 139:13, Isaiah 46:10)

How comforting is that to know? When we don't know the answer, God does! He *allowed* these health, money, and relational issues to come into our lives. There is a purpose in all of it. One day all will be revealed. His plan will unfold gently and beautifully—like the petals of a flower. The illuminated path will shine; we will clearly see and exclaim, "Aha!" Why had I not seen that before? But it was there the entire time. We were looking through foggy glasses, and God will clear the fog, and our vision will be 20/20.

What a glorious day that will be!

Abbott and Costello

Ron's birthday arrived, and I didn't have high hopes of being able to renew his driver's license. I put it into God's hands, rationalizing he could always get state issued identification.

We headed to the Bureau of Motor Vehicles (DMV). This is always a fun chore, but especially when you're wading into unfamiliar waters. Once someone has driven their entire lives and may now be denied, it creates a tense situation. Especially for a man who's always been in charge.

Ron remembered the name of a lady who had taken care of him in the past. Her name was Lydia, so we asked specifically for her to take care of us. Fortunately, she was working that day and they escorted us right back.

We sat in front of Lydia's desk and Ron jabbered away, attempting to make conversation with her, but making no sense. I tensed up, silently wishing he would keep quiet. Lydia didn't seem fazed, and said, "Let's first do the eye test."

God help us.

"Put your eye up to the machine and read me the first line," she said.

Ron started speed reading. She said, "Slow down, slow down."

He asked, "Which one do you want?"

She repeated, "Read line 1."

He finally got through line 1. Tentatively, she passed him. One test down. Several to go.

She said, "Come back on Monday." We needed to provide some documents, and now had the weekend to ponder everything.

Monday arrived and we headed back to the DMV. He didn't have to take the eye exam again, but still had some questions to answer.

She asked, "Have you ever been convicted of selling drugs?"

Ron nodded and smiled, "Yes!"

I shook my head vigorously side to side. "No, you haven't!"

Fixing his eyes on me, he said, "Nooooo...," shaking instead of nodding.

Several more questions went on exactly the same way.

"Are you diabetic?" she asked.

"Yes!" He said, smiling and nodding again.

"No!" I countered. He looked at me and quickly changed from nodding to shaking again. Then he said, "No."

Frazzled, we finally made it through the questions. He got his picture taken, and we walked out with a brand new driver's license in hand. Good for another eight more years.

PART II

30 Years Ago

Thirty years ago Ron and I met under seemingly divine circumstances. I lived in Cincinnati, the single mother of a young daughter, Molly, two and a half. I'm not proud to say I wasn't living a good life, moving from relationship to relationship—looking for love. And love in all the wrong places. The man I lived with was cruel and deviant, but I found out much too late.

It was Christmas. Things between us had deteriorated to the point where I was desperate, not knowing where to turn or how to get out of the relationship. My sister, Sharon, invited me and my daughter to visit her family in Indianapolis, so I jumped at the chance to escape him and think. As I drove away from the city and pulled onto the interstate, my burden lifted. I prayed but wasn't sure God heard my prayers, as all seemed silent. There seemed to be no solution as to how to leave this man.

We pulled up in front of my sister's small white house, and once we settled in, I explained everything. Later that evening, my brother-in-law (at the time), informed me he and his cousin were picking up a moving truck and moving me out of that apartment. Matt said I was going to live with them.

I protested, "But what about my job?"

"Forget the job. "You're not going back," he said.

With no fight left in me, I smiled weakly and agreed. Knowing my daughter and I were now safe, I went straight to bed, sleeping through the night and most of the next day—which happened to be Super Bowl XXIII Sunday.

That evening, Sharon and Matt were going out and asked me to tag along, since they'd hired a babysitter to watch the kids. However, I didn't want to go anywhere or do anything. I felt depleted, but despite my protests, my family was persistent and wouldn't take no for an answer. I gave in.

Back then, Chi Chi's Mexican Restaurants were still in operation. A bar operated separately from the restaurant with a big screen television and free hors d'oeuvres along the back wall. The Super Bowl played on a big screen TV, so our plan was to watch the game, have a few drinks, eat some free food, and go home. But that's not what happened.

I sat on one side of the dimly lit bar with my sister. My sociable brother-in-law moved around, talking with everyone in the entire room. He stopped at one point, and I noticed him deep in conversation with a man across the bar. Next thing I knew, Matt appeared by my side and told me he had someone he wanted me to meet.

"No! I don't want to meet anyone," I said.

"Come on," he's a really nice guy. I think you'll like him," he said.

"Fine," I said. Reluctantly, I got up and walked around the corner of the bar. Sitting on the stool, extending his hand to me, sat a giant of a man.

"Hi, I'm Ron, he said.

"Nice to meet you, Ron. I'm Penelope."

Not to be dramatic, but this quick hello between us was like a first meet in the movies. I slipped my hand into his warm one and it fit like a glove. Now, the unknown face now came into sharp focus; a nice face with a boyish grin. When he broke out into a smile, which was often, his entire face lit up.

Also, I didn't know it that night, but Ron had accepted Jesus Christ as his Lord and Savior when he was twelve. I grew up in the Lutheran Church, attended three years of Catechism (a summary of the principles of Christian religion), and church camp. I couldn't tell you the first thing about what I learned during those three years, but felt God's nudge during a week at Camp Mowana while camping, hiking, and singing hymns around a campfire.

The four of us talked for quite a while at Chi Chi's, while cheering on the Cincinnati Bengals, who lost to the San Francisco 49ers. We then decided to go play some darts.

After that night, Ron pursued me with phone calls, flowers and help in the form of research. I was trying to find a new job, and had an interview with the Indiana Pacers professional basketball team. He took time out of his schedule and spent several hours at the library researching the team, players, and management. He compiled all this information for me to review before my interview. I didn't get the job, but he won my heart.

One night, when my sister was distressed, he prayed with her. I also bowed my head at the same time and asked Jesus Christ to come into my heart and save me. I turned my life over to his control and never looked back.

We married and have now been together now for over 30 years, and it's never been boring!

Ron's Nine Lives

During our lifetime, we may have a brush with death or perhaps only the final encounter. This was not Ron's first encounter with death and extraordinary detours.

The first instance happened was when he was twelve and attending church camp in Indiana. While swimming in a murky lake, he began to be sucked under by a whirlpool. At the time, he didn't know to relax, lie back, and move away from it. He thrashed, fought and sank deeper into the water's depths until his fight was almost gone. At once, he saw a vision of the flames of hell and a demon's cackling laughter. Before death overtook him, he felt a hand reach down and snatch him out of the water. He gave his life to Jesus Christ that night and never looked back.

Several years before we met, he and a friend were enjoying breakfast at a Kentucky Waffle House when several men started picking a fight. After breakfast, the two left, and the men attacked his friend outside the restaurant. As Ron defended him, someone slipped up behind and slammed a tire iron into his chest. He was sore for several weeks, but actually suffered no broken bones or permanent damage.

Some of his scariest brushes with death were when he had guns pulled on him twice. The first was in Kentucky by greedy and corrupt city officials that wanted a cut of his restaurant business. The second by a man trying to extort money from him at a sporting goods business he managed in Orlando.

Almost 30 years had passed after his first encounter with water, and he was about to experience another. After moving to Florida, we enjoyed taking trips to the ocean. One of our favorite places was New Smyrna Beach—before we found it's one of the worst places in the country for riptides—and sharks. This time, he held our three-year-old daughter and strolled into the ocean waist-deep. In minutes, the chest-high water rose over his head. Shouting, he tried to get my attention, but I didn't realize his distress until I saw Molly climbing on top of his head. Only then did I shout frantically for lifeguards to save them. He was going under and taking on water, so he peeled her off his head and threw her towards the lifeguards. They splashed out to her, plucked her out of the water, and then scooted a paddle board to him. Once his arms were free, he floated on his back and paddled out of the riptide.

Finally, a couple years before the stroke he went into heart failure from an inhaler prescribed for bronchitis, and spent several days in the hospital ICU.

Needless to say, Ron has been a frequent visitor on the road of Extraordinary Detours.

PART III

Memories Return

Since that traumatic day of November 13, 2013, many memories have resurfaced in bits and pieces. There were quite a few things Ron remembered—and many he did not.

Ron remembers lying on our bed, with several strangers gathered around. He remembers multiple voices, and me talking in his ear but not understanding. The muffled sounds bothered him, and he wanted it to stop so he could sleep.

Suddenly, he heard God's voice break through the noise—instructing him to get up. He did as he was told by sitting on the edge of the bed and allowing the EMT's to escort him out the bedroom, into the living room, and onto the stretcher. Although there were two EMT's and three Sheriff's Deputies in the house, not one touched him. He walked by himself into the next room, where they collapsed the stretcher, and he got on by himself. He knew they rolled him out the front door and into the ambulance.

Finally on the way to the hospital, he remembers being covered by a warm blanket—then going unconscious.

However, one memory never changing is the one of his visit to heaven. My curiosity got the best of me and I'd grill him about things I remembered from Citrus Hospital, to Shands, to rehab, and back home again. During the times he'd mention heaven, I'd press for more. Every single time he'd reach the part about glimpsing heaven, he'd cry, choke up, and have to stop. At that point, I'd drop the subject and wait for him to bring it up at another time.

Above all, the biggest puzzle to me, and extremely difficult to comprehend, was the *friend*. First, he showed up in the helicopter, at Shands in the ER, and then again in the neurology ward. Repeatedly throughout the years, we discussed the friend and his significance, before I finally felt comfortable enough to share.

Was it Jesus? Was it an angel? Was it someone you did or didn't know? What did they look like? Sound like? These were my questions, and I'm sure yours, as well.

I'll now share Ron's *friend* with you—as he relayed the details to me.

The Friend

Ron's *friend* is a mystery which I'll attempt to unravel. But first, let's take a little detour to the dollar store, where we'll purchase a box or bag jigsaw puzzle. The picture on the outside may be a cat, flower, cartoon, or landscape. That's how the finished piece will look when you complete it. When you get the puzzle home and open the bag or box, you scatter the pieces and put them back together again. If you lose a piece, your puzzle is now incomplete and the picture won't be completely filled in.

Now, imagine with me for a moment. Close your eyes and picture your physical body as a finished puzzle. If you have a full length mirror, go stand in front of it. Marvel at the magnificent body given to you by God. The only thing you see reflected in the mirror is the physical body. However, that's not all there is. Your human body, from head to toe, and everything inside is the entire puzzle. Now, we're going to break open the box and scatter the pieces. Your human body is divided up into three distinct puzzle pieces:

Body
Soul
Spirit

#1 Puzzle Piece is the body. We all have a body. That is a given while we're here on this earth.

#2 Puzzle Piece is the soul. The soul is touched by music, books, movies, and other people.

#3 Puzzle Piece is the one missing for a lot of people. We're incomplete until we receive the most important puzzle piece of all. That is:

- Father
- Son
- Holy Spirit

#3 is the *Spirit.* The third puzzle piece is *three-inside-one piece.* God the Father, God the Son, and God the Holy Spirit.

While Ron was inside the helicopter, laid out on a stretcher, his physical body was dying. However, his friend was with him the entire time. Once he was in the hospital, he remembers friends coming to visit, but he said hello and went to sleep. Soon afterward, he was outside of the hospital, eight floors up, looking inside windows at his body and friends standing by his bedside.

His friend was his soul.

His friend the Spirit (3-in-1) was also with him.

His body was separated into three distinct pieces: Body, Soul and Spirit.

His puzzle pieces separated, and he could see them clearly. They were three separate people carrying on a conversation, but they were all Ron—the entire puzzle.

In the Bible, Paul the Apostle attempted to describe his own extraordinary detour—similar to Ron's. Awestruck by sights and sounds he experienced, he tried to explain as follows:

"It is doubtless not profitable for me to boast. I will come to visions and revelations of the Lord. I know a man in Christ who fourteen years ago—whether in the body I do not know, or whether out of the body I do not know, God knows—such a one was caught up to the third heaven. And I know such a man—whether in the body or out of the body I do not know, God knows—how he was caught up into Paradise and heard inexpressible words, which it is not lawful for man to utter. Of such a one I will boast, yet of myself I will not boast, except in my infirmities. For though I might desire to boast, I will not be a fool, for I will speak the truth. But I refrain, lest anyone should think of me above what he sees me to be or hears from me."

2 Corinthians 12:1-6 (NKJV)

The Roman Road

You may be wondering after reading Ron's story, how you, too, may enter into the kingdom of heaven. I would be remiss if I did not share God's plan of salvation.

"In the beginning, God created the heavens and the earth."
Genesis 1:1, KJV

He created them for us, his children, but we must also do certain things as well. As He is our Heavenly Father, he loves us and wanted us to rule and live on the earth as long as we are alive. And then, at our time of death, He wants to bring us into His Heaven to live forever with Him. God's way is His free gift of salvation through Jesus Christ.

So, how in the world can you get to heaven?

The simplest way to understanding is called *The Roman Road to Salvation.* The Roman Road is a collection of verses in Paul's Epistle to the Romans, offering a clear and structured path to Jesus Christ. A road *map*, if you will.

With this in mind, many people believe if they're a good person, they're automatically offered a free pass through heaven's door. They truly may have done good things, like going to church their entire lives, getting baptized, and perhaps even doing charity work. However, the Bible declares no one is perfect.

"As it is written, there is none righteous, no not one." Roman 3:10 (NKJV)

Therefore, we need a road to God that relies on His gift of grace, and not on something we or anyone else can do. Otherwise, we'd surely brag about how our works got us there—and not the divine work of God. God's way is that He conquers death with life. The life, death, burial, and resurrection of God's Son, the Lord Jesus Christ.

There's a quote mostly attributed mostly to Benjamin Franklin that says, *Nothing is sure in life except death and taxes.* I bet you make sure to pay your taxes every year, but what about your home after death? Do you know where you're going?

Accordingly, if you follow this map to eternal salvation with God, you'll be assured of your eternal home when you die. These verses will answer the following questions for you:

Who needs salvation?
Why do they need it?
How does God provide it?
How do we receive it?
What are the results?

Dig out your dusty Bible, borrow one from a friend or the library, or purchase a paperback copy. Then, look up and read each of the following five scriptures one by one, in the order listed. I've referenced the NIV (New International Version), but you can use the version you understand best. Then follow the action items in the form of a prayer after you read the verses.

The Romans Road

1. **Romans 3:23** - For all have sinned and fall short of the glory of God.

DO: *Admit that you are a sinner.*

2. **Romans 5:8** - But God demonstrates his own love for us in this: While we were still sinners, Christ died for us.

DO: Believe in your heart that God sent Jesus Christ to die on the cross to save you from sin and death.

3. **Romans 6:23** - For the wages of sin is death, but the gift of God is eternal life in Christ Jesus our Lord.

DO: Understand that as a sinner, you and I deserve nothing less than death.

4. **Romans 8:1** - Therefore, there is now no condemnation for those who are in Christ Jesus.

DO: Repent, which means to turn from your old life of sin to a new life in Christ.

5. **Romans 10:9** - That if you confess with your mouth, "Jesus is Lord," and believe in your heart that God raised him from the dead, you will be saved.

DO: Receive God's free gift of salvation through faith in Jesus Christ.

Here's the prayer put together:

God, I admit that I'm a sinner. I now know there is nothing I can do to save myself. I believe that you sent Jesus to die on the cross for my sins. I repent and turn now from my sins, and ask for your forgiveness. I would like to put my faith in Jesus and receive your free gift of salvation. Thank you for forgiving me, saving me, and taking me to heaven with you when I die. Amen.

God knows our heart, and if you prayed through each one of those verses, and believed that Jesus Christ died for your sins, then you are saved! You are now a part of the family of God, and will see Him when you die.

In summary, continue to read your Bible. Spend a little time with God each day, praying and reading His Word. Ask Him to increase your faith and understanding. And He will! Start with the Book of John and read about the life, death, burial and resurrection of Jesus. Then start at the beginning in Genesis, and read straight through to Revelation, so you can grasp the Old and New Testaments and 66 books of the Bible. Try to find a local church, where you will be part of a body of local believers who will come beside you on your journey. Ask the pastor about getting baptized, which shows your commitment to Jesus Christ.

Let us know if you prayed this prayer and became a believer in Jesus. We'd love to welcome you personally into the family of God.

Horse in the Road

Ron's soul and spirit were to take another trip in February of 2017.

In the early morning hours, he was driving a stretch of dark country road to fetch donuts. The countryside was misty, quiet and still, when a horse appeared in the road. He couldn't stop in time.

Previously, another car before him had hit the horse and veered off the road into a tree, which fell on top of his car. The horse was still in the road, and attempting to stand when Ron drove right over it. He recalled that it felt like driving over a refrigerator. His left front tire blew out, and the airbag exploded in his face, pushing him into the door. Miraculously, his glasses were not shattered on his face. The impact lifted the Chrysler Pacifica, spun it around, and landed it on the side of the road—pointing towards home.

Although disoriented, Ron still managed to call me. He said, "Honey, there's a horse in the road today." I couldn't believe it was a horse, and asked him if it was a cow. Then the line went dead. He'd snapped the phone shut and gone unconscious.

Ambulances, fire trucks, and State Highway Patrol came screaming onto the scene. This bizarre accident, involving a horse and two vehicles, shut down the entire stretch of road in both directions.

At some time in the future, Ron opened his eyes to people in his face again, shooting questions at him. Because of his aphasia, he couldn't comprehend and answer their questions, so they suspected a brain injury. He did get thumped in the head, which gave him a concussion. In order to get him quickly to the hospital, the EMT's dispatched a helicopter.

In less than thirty minutes, it landed in the middle of the road, and he was shuffled onto a helicopter for the second time in less than four years. Aboard the helicopter, his body, soul, and spirit separated again.

His friend (soul and spirit) peered out of the helicopter windows to see if anyone else was hurt. Then, he fell into total darkness.

PART IV – *June 2014*

The Newspaper Ad

It was now June, seven months past Ron's stroke, and hot enough to fry an egg on the sidewalk. We were holed up inside the house with nothing to do. Bored, I leafed through our small town paper when a full-page, color ad caught my eye:

Seeking post-menopausal women for clinical research study on hot flashes. New medication and compensation provided for qualified applicants.

Free Q & A session and lunch provided. Medical doctor on site to answer questions. Call 352-555-HOTFLASH to make your appointment.

Free lunch. Great bait. "Honey, take a look at this." I passed the paper to my husband. He had made remarkable strides in healing, and we had learned to communicate—somewhat. I held my breath, waiting. "Well, what do you think?"

He scanned the ad, his eyes opening wide, and returned the paper. "Food, right?"

Relieved, I folded the paper and closed my eyes, rapidly fanning tiny beads of perspiration forming on my brow. Hot dog! All my troubles will be over and I'll sweat no more. *A gift sent straight from heaven.* Grabbing a pad, I jotted down the phone number to call first thing on Monday.

Excitement kept my eyes open most of the night. At dawn, I rolled out of bed, dressed quickly and flipped the switch on the coffee maker. I kept an eye on the clock until it flipped over to nine a.m.

A perky receptionist answered, "Naturecoast Clinical Research, how may I help you?"

"Yes, this is Penelope Silvers. I'd like to sign up for the free hot flash lunch session."

"Great! I've got you down."

Inhaling deeply, I plunged in, "Oh, and could my husband tag along? We can bring his lunch." I explained how he'd suffered a stroke, and didn't like to be far from me.

"Of course he may come," she said. "We'll have enough food for both of you." Sighing my thanks, I hung up; grateful he could attend so I wouldn't have to worry. One less thing on my plate.

Hot Flash Study

The day of our briefing dawned hot and muggy. We arrived at the office, and a nurse ushered our tiny group into a compact conference room—a plump brunette, a freckled redhead who constantly fanned and wiped her brow, my husband and me.

We sat at the end of a long, oblong table. Clipboards holding blank medical release forms were passed around, and we began penning in information as the doctor spoke. He said, "All medical tests will be provided. Before you're accepted into this triple blind study you'll get a complete physical."

Each of us received a hot flash diary, and from this point on we were known only by our subject initials and subject number. Keeping track of sweats from mild, moderate, severe, to none was to be our assignment.

Famished, and reeling from digesting heaps of information, we were given the green light to rip open bulging brown paper sack lunches and dive into our lunch of turkey subs, chips, cookie and drinks.

First, we had to make it through all the medical tests before being given the green light. Staff crammed appointments into one day, wanting to quickly start me on either a placebo or the test medication. Blood work was going to be difficult. My veins are tiny and tend to roll away from needles. I informed Sherrie, the nurse, she'd end up using my hand. That's exactly where she headed after bruising up both arms. My blood was sludgy (their words) on this day, so she gave me (and herself) some needed relief and sent me off for test number two.

Next test was done quickly, and finally, the mammogram. I considered backing out since a mammogram four years prior nearly caused me to black out. However, as was my second attempt with an accounting class after college, this was a piece of cake. Results would come back in about forty-eight hours, so we left for home and I put it out of my mind.

Pass or Fail

The phone rang several days later. Sherrie said the radiologist had expressed some concern about abnormalities on my mammogram. "You need to return to Dr. Scott's office so he can review the film and repeat the exam." She assured me, "We've seen these things before. Don't worry about it; it's usually nothing."

Quickly, we scheduled another appointment. As I sat on the cold examination table, the doctor said, "I can't feel any lumps here."

Partly relieved he may have made a mistake; I paused for an awkward moment, and then corrected him. "Um, doc, the other breast."

Flustered, he said, "Oh, sorry," then moved to the left.

Just as before, no lumps were found; and I had no symptoms. He pointed to the X-ray film and said, "See these spots? They appear as tiny grains of sand, called micro-calcifications. I'd like to refer you to an oral surgeon for further testing."

Repeating the process again, the surgeon, Dr. Rhodes, checked me over but couldn't detect anything. He said, "I'd like to schedule you for a biopsy at the hospital just to rule anything out."

Fear turned my hot flashes to ice. My voice stuck in my throat. "How do you perform a biopsy?"

"We go into the breast with a very thin needle in a couple different locations and extract out a sample of the affected tissue." I cringed as he continued. "Testing the tissue will rule out any possibility of cancer," he said. Dr. Rhodes held my hand. "You did great. Call my office in about two weeks for the results."

I recalled Sherrie's words, *it's nothing. Most of these are benign.* Calm and peace flooded over me again. I knew many others were praying for me. *Benign and fine.* This was now my motto.

Into the Abyss

Surgery now loomed for the first time in my life. Steeling myself for what lay ahead, I wanted a clean bill of health and my life back. I'd enjoyed robust health—not even a broken bone—for fifty-four years.

On the day of my autopsy, prayers flew to heaven. A team of four nurses, alongside the doctor, were waiting for me inside the tiny operating room. Shivering, I laid face down on the table with my breast through a cut-out hole, and *The Lord is my Shepherd, I shall not want,* running through my head. A nurse covered me with a warm blanket and gently placed her hand on my back. Cold sweat poured from my body. Quickly, the procedure was over and I was wheeled back to the recovery room.

The Verdict

The day arrived for my appointment with Dr. Rhodes. Strong incense and new age music assaulted my nose and ears as we entered his office. Agitated, I forced deep belly breaths to calm myself. A young girl peered at me behind a glass window, cracked it open and shoved a sign-in sheet my way, quickly averting her eyes.

While my husband sat quietly by my side in the sparsely furnished waiting room, I was thankful we were alone. Attempting a distraction, I picked up a magazine and flipped through a Reader's Digest, *30 Tips*...the words blurring.

Soon after, I heard my name.

"Penelope Silvers?"

"Yes. I'm here." I tossed my magazine on the table and met the nurse at the door. We followed her to a room, and she said the doctor would be right in. Silence was deafening, enhancing the tick ticking of the clock.

Finally, Dr. Rhodes made an entrance. Barely sitting, he blurted, "Unfortunately, it's cancer, looks like stage one. We caught it early."

Overwhelmed, my body turned numb and I couldn't breathe. *This can't be real. I'd been so sure—everyone so sure—nothing was wrong. We were all wrong.*

The doctor was talking, talking, talking. Bits and pieces of his voice floated on the air. "Lumpectomy...Mastectomy...Surgery..." He held papers in front of me full of pictures and words, circling things. "Do you have any questions?" he asked.

There were no words for what I was feeling, so I shook my head no. Glancing at Ron, I could see he was a total wreck. It was clear we needed to escape as quickly as possible to process this new information.

Meanwhile, the doctor touched my shoulder and said, "I'm here if you need me. We'll work on this together. Make sure to leave your information with the office manager. She'll have a local oncologist call you to set up an appointment, and devise a treatment plan for you. I'll be in touch."

Ron and I plopped down on a couch outside of the room for a minute so he could pull himself together. I consoled him and patted his arm. "Everything will be alright, honey. Don't worry." I wasn't so sure.

Next, we stopped by the front desk and left my information for the next doctor to call me. Stumbling out the door into bright daylight, my husband began crying. I did the one thing I've been doing for the last nine months—I took charge.

Pulling him close, I said, "Listen, we can get through this just like we got through the stroke. Don't you think God knows all about this? There's nothing to fear. At least, now we know and can make some plans."

Finally climbing into the car, we sat in silence for a few minutes as cars buzzed up and down the highway. People went about their day, just as we had moments before the news. Now everything had changed, and it was time to make life and death decisions. Again.

And he said…"The Lord gave, and the Lord has taken away; blessed be the name of the Lord." Job 1:21 (NKJV)

God is Near

After many tears and sleepless nights later, we made the decision to go to Moffitt Cancer Hospital in Tampa. My breast cancer was stage two, HER3+, a very aggressive type of cancer. I had a simple mastectomy on November 15, 2014, almost a year to the day of Ron's stroke and trip to heaven. After surgery, the oncologist recommended chemotherapy to eradicate any stray cancer cells floating throughout my body.

I've heard it said God is closest in the midst of the storms, and I can fully testify to this. During the next year and a half, I felt God's presence and His angels surrounding and protecting us like never before.

To illustrate, on my first day of surgery we woke about three a.m. to make the hour and a half trip to Tampa. The air was crisp, and the sky still dark and full of stars. As I waited by the car, I looked up into the heavens and prayed. Calm washed over me, and I felt God's peace and love as He sent me a message. Gazing upward, I saw first one, then two, then three shooting stars, which took my breath away! At that moment, I knew with all my heart I would be okay.

Again, while at Moffitt, we met many different people—those in treatment and the medical personnel doing the treating. Some patients we spoke with were going to be fine, and others were very close to death. One late night after I'd finished with my chemo, we met Jerry and his wife. He was in the chemo chair getting treatment, but they told us it was merely to manage his pain, as he didn't have much longer on this earth. Ron mentioned his trip to heaven, and told Jerry what wondrous things were waiting for him. We asked if we could pray with them, and they agreed. We were blessed to be able to give them a small bit of comfort.

Another time, Ron shared his story with my nurse as she bustled around getting my chemo bags ready. When he shared his story, he'd break down in tears when reaching the part about glimpsing heaven and hearing God's voice. After listening intently, she said, "So, there *really is* a heaven?"

He assured her there was, and talked with her about how to pray and receive Christ. She had never heard anyone share a story like this, and it affected her to the point that she shared it with a hospice patient distraught about dying. She shared with us later that Ron's testimony gave the woman comfort in knowing what was ahead of her.

The entire year of 2015 was spent traveling back and forth every six weeks from Inverness to Tampa. I made it through six rounds of chemotherapy and eighteen treatments of Herceptin, and as far as we knew, the cancer had been eradicated from my body. My future prognosis was good.

In retrospect, we didn't know the cancer had already been growing at the time of Ron's stroke and trip to heaven. Ron drove me back and forth to Moffitt, cooked all the meals, and watched over me as I slept for three straight days. Without a doubt, Ron knew God had sent him back to earth—to care for me.

Oh, in case you're wondering, relief never came for my hot flashes; they're still with me, but I'm alive—all from finding an ad in a newspaper, and making an impulsive decision one hot Sunday afternoon in June.

Proverbs 3:5-6 says, "Trust in the Lord with all your heart, and lean not on your own understanding. In all your ways acknowledge Him, and He will direct your paths.

Mother/Daughter Reunion

While growing up, I had a strained relationship with my mother. I'm not sure if it stemmed from being the oldest, but I felt pressure to do everything right to please her. Keep the perfect room. Dress the perfect way. Talk the perfect way. No backtalk. No sass.

After mom and dad married, he transferred to California where I was born; then Jenny a year later. Three years after they moved back to Ohio, my youngest sister, Sharon, came along. I'm sure I must have been pampered somewhat—being the first. With Jenny I had to share the spotlight, and then Sharon's birth really brought out the green-eyed monster in me, especially when she was born with pneumonia and everyone hovered and whispered over her tent-covered crib. Tension crackled in the air, as a constant stream of doctors filed in and out of the house. Even though only four years old, I knew it was a serious situation. We were unsure whether she'd live or die.

Together with feeling helpless and invisible, I was also angry from this constant attention to my new sister. I've never revealed these feelings or sought out a professional opinion, but perhaps my perfectionist tendencies sprang from that time, as I thought if I behaved perfectly, I'd become the apple of my mother's eye again. Well, that did not happen and just worsened over time.

In addition, my parents' marriage was not a happy one. I didn't know all the details, but knew there wasn't a lot of love. There were never two more different people than my mom and dad. He recently died in 2021, but when alive he was quiet, laid-back, and held everything in. My mom is more of a go-getter and achiever.

Therefore, when she started working, she gained more of her independence from him—and us. After we'd all flown the nest, my mom left home soon after—and things were never the same. Mom moved to Florida to escape my dad and the cold and dreary winters of Ohio. I felt like she'd left us as well.

Soon after, Ron and I also moved to Florida, and secretly I hoped we'd see each other and work on our relationship. We had conversations, but there was never much explanation as to what happened between her and my dad. She married again, and the bitterness furthered darkened my heart when my deepest desires were not fulfilled.

In a fit of fury, I sent my mom a letter and told her I never wanted to see her ever again. And I didn't for nine long years.

While apart, God was working on each of us separately. He was doing a work in my mom, and He was doing a work in me. After several years, I wondered how she was doing, and there was a longing to speak to her, but I didn't know how to go about breaking the silence. I mailed a few cards, but didn't write a return address, still unsure of what I wanted to say. Suffice it to say, God had other plans.

Enter cancer.

After my diagnosis, and sharing the news with my sisters, I received a note from my mom. She'd heard about my cancer through the grapevine, and sent me a short note. The note was poignant and heartfelt. She was grieved to hear of my condition and apologized for anything she'd done to offend me. Those words were like honey to my ears, and I contacted her right away.

Shortly before my surgery we met halfway for breakfast. Awkward at first, we began the slow journey of sharing, and the ice began to thaw around my cold heart. In time, we got to know each other as flawed people—not just mother and daughter. We've been seeing each other and communicating in deeper ways than I ever imagined, and our relationship is the best it's ever been.

Moreover, here's something God showed me during those years apart. Once a root of bitterness takes hold in your heart, it is not from God. This comes straight from the pit of hell, and acts like a cancer needing fed. Even though my mom and I were not talking, there had to be more things in the silence I'd ponder to feed the hatred to keep it alive. God's love is like a rushing waterfall that if allowed in, can wash over you and douse those flames of hell and hate. His love can refresh and revive and heal. God's love is supernatural. Hate consumes you, and eventually those around you. God doesn't force us, but asks us to come and release it all at His feet and begin the healing process. Believe me, it is well worth it and you will never be the same.

In conclusion, if you have your own impossible relationship, don't give up on it, and don't give up on God. He can do a healing work you could never imagine possible.

"With God, all things are possible." Matthew 19:26 (KJV)

Present Day

In just eight short years, God has brought us so far in this journey. Since Ron's trip to heaven, our many extraordinary detours have transformed each of us in ways I would never have imagined. He carried us from sickness to health. He provided peace, love, joy and wisdom. He gave strength when there was none. He brought family back into our lives and supernaturally healed fractured relationships. He gave me a new career to allow us to move forward in confidence towards our senior years.

Sometimes, it helps to write out experiences in a journal and document your life's journey. I've journaled for years, and I'm amazed every time I reflect on God's provisions and His faithfulness to us. He loves us too much to leave us the way we are. I'd like to share just a few of the ways each of us has changed—for the better. For instance:

Ron went from:

Controlling to Easygoing
Decision-maker to Fair-Minded
Disapproving to Appreciative
Harsh to Friendly
Stubborn to Cooperative
Loud to Gentle
Motivated to Mature
Fierce to Calm
Contrary to Supportive
Warrior to Peacemaker

I changed from:

Anxious to Calm
Cowardly to Bold
Depressed to Happy
Distressed to Optimistic
Insecure to Secure
Judgmental to Merciful
Overwhelmed to Focused
Passive to Decisive
Trapped to Imaginative
Unsure to Confident
Vulnerable to Resourceful

When you live through difficult times, God can do a mighty work in you. Sometimes, I believe He puts us in these impossible situations so we look to Him instead of ourselves. Throughout these years, my feeble attempts to completely lean on Him was exactly what He wanted me to do.

The Apostle Paul said, "That is why, for Christ's sake, I delight in weaknesses, in insults, in hardships, in persecutions, in difficulties. For when I am weak, then I am strong." 2 Corinthians 12:10 (NIV)

And finally, because of these trials we experienced, God has blessed us beyond measure with fruits of the Spirit as described in the following verse:

"But the fruit of the Spirit is love, joy, peace, patience, kindness, goodness, faithfulness, gentleness and self-control. Against such things there is no law." Galatians 5:22-23 English Standard Version (ESV)

Conclusion

Think about your life. You never think it's going to be over. You probably believe you'll have plenty of time to fix all your mistakes and make things right with God and people you've wronged. However, one day you wake up and it's over. No more time to talk, no more time to love, no more time to forgive.

The Bible says in James 4:14 that life is "even a vapor that appears for a little time and then vanishes away" (NKJV). I ask you, what are you going to do with the tiny bit of time you have left? God has allowed each of us only so much. What will you do with yours? Because when it's gone, it's gone forever.

The rest of our story, and yours, is still left to be written. You don't have to keep going down the same path you're on right now.

Ask yourself these two questions:

1) What is your life all about?

2) If you died today are you going to heaven?

Ask Jesus to come into your heart today and save you. Don't delay. Your life will never be the same.

"For with the heart one believes unto righteousness, and with the mouth confession is made unto salvation." For the scripture says, "Whoever believes on Him will not be put to shame." For there is no distinction between Jew and Greek, for the same Lord over all is rich to all who call upon him. For "whoever who calls upon the name of Lord shall be saved." Romans 10:10-13 (NKJV)

And if you only remember one thing from our story, remember this:

"For God so loved the world that He gave His only begotten Son, that whoever believes in Him should not perish but have everlasting life. For God did not send His Son into the world to condemn the world, but that the world through Him might be saved."

John 3:16-17 (NKJV)

God loves you!

About the Author

Penelope grew up in a small Midwest town where she enjoyed a good Nancy Drew mystery, dancing to the Jackson 5, and raising bunnies till they chewed their way out to freedom. You'll probably hear her say "pop" for "soda" and the occasional "okie dokie." She despises all things winter, so she and Ron reside in sunny Florida where it never snows and everything is always in bloom.

She's a member of Flourish Writers, James Patterson's Masterclass, and former member of Jerry Jenkins' Writer's Guild—author of the best-selling Left Behind series.

You can find more of Penelope's books available at online retailers. Finally, stay tuned for a new series to follow Extraordinary Detour. You'll read about extraordinary men and women from the Bible, and how God gave them a new direction and purpose.

Ron, Circa 2018